First Biographies

Matthew Henson

by B. A. Hoena

Consulting Editor: Gail Saunders-Smith, PhD
Consultant: The Staff of the Peary-MacMillan Arctic Museum
and Arctic Studies Center
Brunswick, Maine

Capstone
press
Mankato, Minnesota

Pebble Books are published by Capstone Press,
151 Good Counsel Drive, P.O. Box 669, Mankato, Minnesota 56002.
www.capstonepress.com

1 2 3 4 5 6 10 09 08 07 06 05

Library of Congress Cataloging-in-Publication Data
Hoena, B. A.
   Matthew Henson / by B. A. Hoena.
   p. cm.—(Pebble Books. First biographies)
   Summary: "Simple text and photographs describe the life of Matthew Henson,
co-discoverer of the North Pole in 1909"—Provided by publisher.
   Includes bibliographical references and index.
   ISBN 0-7368-5249-2 (hardcover)
   1. Henson, Matthew Alexander, 1866-1955—Juvenile literature. 2. African-
American explorers—Biography—Juvenile literature. 3. North Pole—Discovery
and exploration—Juvenile literature. I. Title. II. Series: First biographies (Mankato,
Minn.)
G635.H4H64 2006
910'.92—dc22   2005001633

Note to Parents and Teachers

The First Biographies set supports national history standards for units on people and culture. This book describes and illustrates the life of Matthew Henson. The images support early readers in understanding the text. The repetition of words and phrases helps early readers learn new words. This book also introduces early readers to subject-specific vocabulary words, which are defined in the Glossary section. Early readers may need assistance to read some words and to use the Table of Contents, Glossary, Read More, Internet Sites, and Index sections of the book.

Table of Contents

Time Line

1866
born

4

Young Matthew

Matthew Henson was born in 1866 in Maryland. His parents died when he was young. Matthew learned to take care of himself.

◄ Washington, D.C., where Matthew's family moved when he was 1 year old

Time Line

1866
born

When he was 12,
Matthew worked on a ship.
The ship's captain taught
him how to read.
He taught Matthew
about history.

◄ a ship much like the one Matthew worked on

Time Line

1866
born

1887
meets explorer
Robert Peary

Exploring the Arctic

At age 21, Matthew met Robert Peary. Robert asked Matthew to work for him. Robert wanted to explore the cold Arctic.

Robert Peary with Matthew (right)

Time Line

1866
born

1887
meets explorer
Robert Peary

1891
sails to
Greenland

In 1891, Matthew and Robert sailed to Greenland. They met Inuit people there. The Inuit helped Matthew and Robert explore the Arctic.

Matthew working with one of his Inuit friends

Time Line

1866
born

1887
meets explorer
Robert Peary

1891
sails to
Greenland

Matthew and Robert made
many trips to the Arctic.
Robert wanted to be
the first person to reach
the North Pole. Robert
needed Matthew's help.

Matthew (right) during an Arctic trip

Time Line

●	●	●
1866 born	1887 meets explorer Robert Peary	1891 sails to Greenland

In 1908, Matthew and Robert hired a group of Inuit. The two men needed help to reach the North Pole. The group used sled dogs for their trip.

Inuit using sled dogs to carry supplies

Time Line

1866	1887	1891
born	meets explorer	sails to
	Robert Peary	Greenland

The trip was long and hard. Matthew, Robert, and the Inuit worked together. On April 6, 1909, they reached the North Pole.

◄ Matthew (center) and four Inuit at the North Pole

1909
reaches the
North Pole

Time Line

1866
born

1887
meets explorer
Robert Peary

1891
sails to
Greenland

After the North Pole

In 1912, Matthew wrote a book about the trip. At first, he did not become famous. Many people did not respect black people at the time.

the cover of Matthew's book

1909
reaches the
North Pole

1912
writes book

Time Line

1866 born	**1887** meets explorer Robert Peary	**1891** sails to Greenland

Finally, Matthew won many medals and awards for his work. He died in 1955. People still remember Matthew's courage.

Matthew receiving a gold medal from the Geographic Society of Chicago in 1948

1909
reaches the
North Pole

1912
writes book

1955
dies

Glossary

Arctic—the area near the North Pole

captain—the person in charge of a ship

courage—the strength to face danger or fear

Greenland—a large island near the North Pole

history—the study of past events

Inuit—people from the Arctic; Inuit were once known as Eskimos.

North Pole—the northern-most point on Earth; the North Pole is in the Arctic.

respect—to admire and have a good opinion of someone

Read More

Armentrout, David, and Patricia Armentrout. *Matthew Henson.* Discover the Life of an American Legend. Vero Beach, Fla.: Rourke, 2004.

Gaines, Ann. *Matthew Henson and the North Pole Expedition.* Journey to Freedom. Chanhassen, Minn: Child's World, 2001.

Hoena, B. A. *Matthew Henson: Arctic Adventurer.* Graphic Library: Graphic Biographies. Mankato, Minn.: Capstone Press, 2006.

Internet Sites

FactHound offers a safe, fun way to find Internet sites related to this book. All of the sites on FactHound have been researched by our staff.

Here's how:

1. Visit *www.facthound.com*

2. Type in this special code **0736852492** for age-appropriate sites. Or enter a search word related to this book for a more general search.

3. Click on the **Fetch It** button.

FactHound will fetch the best sites for you!

Index

Word Count: 207
Grades: 1–2
Early-Intervention Level: 18

Editorial Credits
Mari C. Schuh, editor; Heather Kindseth, set designer; Patrick D. Dentinger,
  book designer; Kelly Garvin, photo researcher/photo editor

Photo Credits
Corbis/Bettmann, cover, 16, 20
Dartmouth College Library, Rauner Special Collections Library, 10, 14
Getty Images Inc./Hulton Archive, 4, 6
Invisible Cities Press, 18
Library of Congress, 1, 12
Special Collections Library, University of Michigan, 8